REAL HEROES

STORIES ABOUT
SURVIVING
HIV/AIDS

Theresa Saliba

W
FRANKLIN WATTS
LONDON • SYDNEY

First published in 2010 by Franklin Watts

Franklin Watts
338 Euston Road
London NW1 3BH

Franklin Watts Australia
Level 17/207 Kent Street, Sydney, NSW 2000

Produced by Arcturus Publishing Limited, 26/27 Bickels Yard, 151–153 Bermondsey Street, London SE1 3HA

Series concept: Alex Woolf
Editor and picture research: Alex Woolf
Designer: Ian Winton

Picture Credits
Corbis: cover and 27 (Louise Gubb), 6 (Bettmann), 7 (Gideon Mendel), 9 (Gideon Mendel), 11 (Gideon Mendel), 12–13 (Roy McMahon), 14 (Roy McMahon), 15 (Michael Brennan), 18–19 (RelaXimages), 20 (Gideon Mendel), 22–23 (Gideon Mendel), 24 (Gideon Mendel), 25 (Gideon Mendel), 28–29 (Jose Luis Pelaez), 30 (Jose Luis Pelaez), 31 (Image Source), 32–33 (Comstock), 34 (Comstock), 35 (Comstock), 36 (Adrian Burke), 37 (Hugh Patrick Brown/Sygma), 40, 41, 43 (Bloom Image).
Getty Images: 39 (Hulton Archive).
Science Photo Library: 8 (Thomas Deerinck, NCMIR).
Shutterstock: 16–17 (VojtechVlk), 21 (Tom Prokop).

Cover picture: A 15-year-old orphaned girl living in Mwaiseni, Zambia, with her two-year-old daughter. Seventy per cent of the world's HIV/AIDS victims live in southern Africa. Millions of orphaned children are left to care for themselves after their parents have succumbed to the disease.

Every attempt has been made to clear copyright. Should there be any inadvertent omission, please apply to the publisher for rectification.

The author would like to acknowledge the following sources:
Books
The First Year: HIV - An Essential Guide for the Newly Diagnosed by D Berger (Marlowe & Co, 2007); *BMA A-Z Family Medical Encyclopedia* (Dorling Kindersley, 2004); *The Cure for HIV and AIDS: With Over 75 Case Histories* by H Clark (New Century Press, 1993); *HIV and AIDS in Africa: Beyond Epidemiology* by E Kalipeni, S Craddock, J Oppong and J Ghosh (Wiley-Blackwell, 2003); *HIV Essentials* by P Sax (Jones and Bartlett Publishers, 2008); *And the Band Played On: Politics, People, and the AIDS Epidemic* by R Shilts (St Martins Press, 2007).

Websites
www.avert.org
www.aids.org
www.hiv.com
www.aidsalliance.org
www.freedomhealth.co.uk
www.aidsmap.com

www.who.int/hiv
www.hiv.lanl.gov
www.aidsarchive.com
www.aidsinfo.nih.gov
www.mihivnews.com
www.ohpe.ca

A CIP catalogue record for this book is available from the British Library.

Dewey Decimal Classification Number: 362.1'969792'00922

ISBN 978 1 4451 0070 8

Printed in China

Franklin Watts is a division of Hachette Children's Books, an Hachette UK company.
www.hachette.co.uk

SL001050EN

Contents

Introduction 6

Ani's Story – Zimbabwe 10
Jake's Story – United States 12
Coco's Story – France 16
Wayne's Story – United Kingdom 18
Ebenezer's Story – South Africa 22
Mala's Story – Zambia 26
Claudia's Story – Honduras 28
Matthew's Story – United States 32
JD's Story – United States 36
Manu's Story – Australia 40
Lian's Story – Singapore 42

Glossary 44
Further Information 45
Index 46

Introduction

HIV stands for human immunodeficiency virus. A virus is a tiny microorganism that invades the cells of other organisms, such as animals and humans, and causes them to become ill. If people are infected by the HIV virus, they are said to be HIV positive (HIV+). The HIV virus is particularly serious because it can cause the immune system to fail. The immune system is a system of cells, tissues and organs that defends the body against attacks. It defends the body against germs and microorganisms and so protects us against disease.

What is AIDS?

AIDS stands for acquired immune deficiency syndrome. It is a disease of the human immune system caused by the HIV virus. AIDS develops if a person who is HIV+ does not receive treatment early enough. AIDS is not a single disease: it is a condition that occurs when a person's immune system has been weakened by HIV so much that he or she is unable to fight off any infection or disease. Cancer, pneumonia and other illnesses are more likely to take hold in AIDS sufferers because of their weakened immune systems.

How does HIV/AIDS spread?

The HIV infection cannot spread through the air, like a cold, or by skin-to-skin contact with another person. For someone to

◄ **At a press conference on 23 April 1984, Dr Robert Gallo, a researcher at the National Cancer Institute, and Margaret Heckler, the US Health Secretary, announce that the HIV virus has been identified. Gallo led the American team that made the discovery.**

Where did HIV/AIDS come from?

The first cases of AIDS occurred in the United States in 1981. Nobody knew what caused it. In 1984 scientists in France and the United States identified the HIV virus as the cause of AIDS. Since then scientists have discovered what the virus looks like and how it attacks the body. However, they do not know where it comes from or how it originally started to infect humans. Many scientists believe that it was around for at least 20 years before it was discovered.

become infected by HIV, their bodily fluids must mix with the bodily fluids of an HIV+ person. There are various ways this can happen.

- The most common way for HIV to spread is through unprotected sexual intercourse. This can be avoided through abstinence, faithfulness in a lasting relationship or by practising safe sex.
- In the early days of HIV/AIDS, people who received blood transfusions often became infected with HIV. Today, in developed countries, this is rare, as blood is routinely screened before use to make sure it is not HIV+. In some developing countries, however, blood is not screened for HIV and therefore infections still occur in this way.

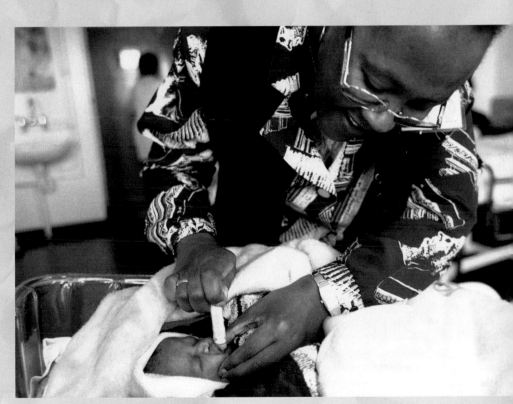

▲ A newborn baby in Cape Town, South Africa, whose mother is HIV+, is given a dose of a drug called Nerirapine. If a mother is given a dose during labour and her baby is treated after birth, the chance of the virus passing from mother to child is greatly reduced. However, because of the high cost, these drugs are not widely available in developing countries.

- HIV can pass from mother to child during the last weeks of pregnancy, or during a normal birth. The risk can be greatly reduced if the mother is given drug treatment during pregnancy, and if the baby is born by caesarean section.
- Drug addicts who share needles also risk HIV infection.

Symptoms of HIV/AIDS

The HIV infection has four stages: an incubation period, acute infection, latency stage and AIDS. The incubation period does not have any particular symptoms and lasts between two and four weeks. The second stage, acute infection, lasts around four weeks and the symptoms include fever, swollen lymph nodes (often under the arm or in the neck or groin), a sore throat and extreme tiredness. The latency stage comes next and shows few or no symptoms. The final stage is AIDS. People do not die of AIDS but of the conditions that result from a weakened immune system because of HIV. People with AIDS will often show symptoms such as fevers, sweats (particularly at night), swollen glands, chills, weakness and weight loss.

Treating HIV/AIDS

Medicines known as antiretroviral (ARV) drugs are available to treat people diagnosed as being HIV+. These medicines suppress the virus and stop it from multiplying in the body, but there is as yet no known cure. A common approach to treating HIV/AIDS is known as HAART (highly active antiretroviral therapy). Patients take a mixture of several (usually three or four) ARV drugs

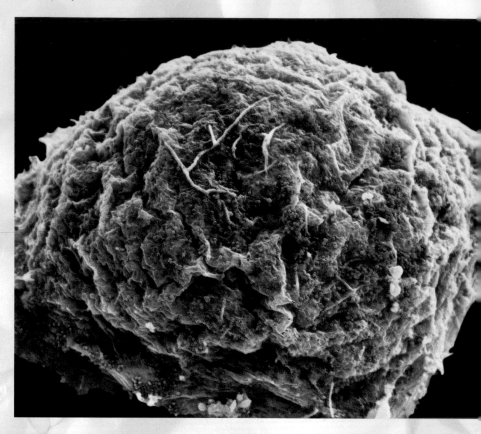

▲ This is a highly magnified picture of a white blood cell infected with HIV, seen here as red dots. White blood cells fight disease as part of the immune system. The virus enters the cell and makes copies of itself, visible here as they come to the surface of the white cell. The cell is destroyed, severely weakening the immune system and causing AIDS.

What parts of the world are affected by HIV/AIDS?

HIV/AIDS particularly affects sub-Saharan Africa, but is also very common in South Asia. In 2007 an estimated 33.2 million people suffered from the disease worldwide, of which 22.5 million lived in sub-Saharan Africa. South Africa has the largest population of HIV patients in the world, followed by Nigeria and India.

to stabilize their symptoms and to reduce the amount of virus in their body. This can improve their general health and increase their survival time.

ARV drugs are very expensive and need to be taken for the rest of a person's life. Many HIV/AIDS patients can't afford the drugs, especially in developing countries where they are desperately needed. Without treatment, about nine out of every ten people with HIV will develop AIDS after 10–15 years. Health organizations working in developing countries are trying to tackle HIV by trying to stop people from becoming infected in the first place. They promote measures such as safe sex and needle-exchange programmes (to encourage drug addicts not to share needles) in attempts to slow the spread of the virus.

Real life heroes

This book tells the stories of some young people who have had personal experience of HIV/AIDS, either through becoming infected themselves or through losing loved ones to the disease. Their courage and determination in the face of tremendous suffering and loss is a testament to the human spirit. The stories are all true, but people's names and some aspects of their identities have been changed.

▶ **ARV treatment is the key to fighting the spread of HIV infection and reducing the risk of AIDS. This young South African woman is having a blood test to check her immune system. Six years ago, she was very ill with AIDS and close to death. Now she is much happier and healthier thanks to the ARV treatment she has received from the Siyaphila La (We are Living Here) HIV treatment project. In 2008 the number of people in South Africa infected with HIV/AIDS reached 5.2 million.**

Ani's Story
Zimbabwe

Ani was seven years old when she found out her father was HIV+. She didn't understand what HIV was but she knew her father, Kundi, was sick. Kundi had been ill for some time and had struggled to care for Ani and her three brothers and sisters since their mother died three years previously.

Ani was playing on the streets of Harare in Zimbabwe one day when she was spotted by a local AIDS charity worker, who thought she was very young to be wandering the streets alone. The charity worker asked Ani where she lived and Ani took her to meet her father. Realizing how ill he was, the charity worker arranged for Kundi to go to hospital so he could start on a course of ARV drugs.

While Kundi was in hospital, Ani and her brothers and sisters were cared for by an aunt. She made sure they went to school and cooked them a meal each day. Ani and her family were lucky – many children have to give up school to care for a sick parent or relative. In Ani's case, she was able to stay at school with the support of her family.

When Kundi was well enough to leave hospital, he was given information about HIV and told how to control his illness. His employer kept his job open until he was well enough to return to work. Although Ani is now only nine, each day after school she collects water from a local well and takes care of her brothers and sisters until her father returns from work.

Kundi finds it difficult to get the medicines he needs but he has been helped by the local AIDS charity. He knows it is important that his children eat properly but this is a challenge. Kundi barely earns enough to feed his family, so Ani helps him grow pumpkins and squash on a small piece of land at the back of their house. They try to sell the excess to buy food and medicines.

HIV/AIDS in Zimbabwe

In Zimbabwe, one in seven adults have HIV and approximately one person becomes infected every three minutes. Zimbabwe also has the world's highest number of AIDS orphans, in proportion to its population. More than 17,000 Zimbabwean children are infected with HIV each year, most through mother-to-child transmission. Nevertheless, there are signs of positive changes. Condom use has increased. Education campaigns have targeted young people, and awareness of HIV/AIDS is higher than average for sub-Saharan Africa.

Ani and her father realize the importance of good nutrition, basic hygiene and a healthy lifestyle. Ani is doing well at school and wants to be a doctor when she is older. She knows this will be a challenge because they are so poor, but she is determined to help others in her community.

▶ Although she is very young, Ani helps her father each day by collecting water from a local well. While her father is at work, she cares for her younger brothers and sisters. Many young people with HIV+ parents must become responsible for doing the housework, caring for younger sisters and brothers and for sick or dying parents. Research in Kenya has shown that children of HIV+ parents are less likely to attend school than other children.

Jake's Story
United States

Jake is 11 years old and lives in California. He has had a very tough life for such a young boy. He lost both his parents to HIV/AIDS. His father died two years ago from AIDS-related cancer and his mother died from AIDS-related pneumonia a year later. Thankfully, Jake is not infected with HIV.

Jake misses his parents very much. 'I miss doing things with them. I used to go shopping with my mom, or sometimes we'd go to the movies. She was great fun to be with. I remember my dad being a lot sicker than mom and he didn't always have the energy to do things with me. But we spent time together, working on school projects or he would tell me stories – I really miss him too.'

Although Jake lives with his aunt and uncle, it's not the same. 'There are lots of little things I miss about them, like just talking to my mom, telling her what went on at school, asking her to help with my homework, that sort of thing. I could talk over my problems with her and she understood – I don't have that with anyone else.'

The first time his parents told them about their illness, Jake was seven years old. He didn't really understand what HIV or AIDS were, but he remembers his parents were 'different' from his friends' parents. They were often tired and had to rest throughout the day. Jake also remembers the doctor visiting the house regularly, but he wasn't fully aware of what was happening. Sometimes they were really sick and his aunt would come to help out around the house.

It was the uncertainty that really affected Jake. 'I remember my dad telling me that they were really poorly and he told me to be strong. He warned me that they could deteriorate quite quickly. I never knew how long they would be with me – months or years – I just didn't know. I used to worry all the time, wondering if they would still be there when I got up in the morning or when I came home from school.'

▶ Jake remembers how his father used to feel tired during the day and sometimes would rest his head on Jake's knee. Jake would tell his father about his day, what he did at school and the things he learned. Jake enjoyed these times, but often wished his dad had more energy like other dads.

Dealing with the stigma of HIV/AIDS

It is difficult for a young person to confide in friends if a family member is HIV+ or has AIDS. Jake didn't tell anyone about his parents' illness because he was worried that his friends would think he was infected too. He wasn't able to tell anyone how worried he was about his parents so he kept his feelings to himself, which made him feel very lonely. People can often miss out on getting the advice and support they need because of the stigma attached to HIV and AIDS. It is important to speak to someone such as a teacher, a youth worker or another trusted adult. They can offer support and practical advice, or point out where to find it.

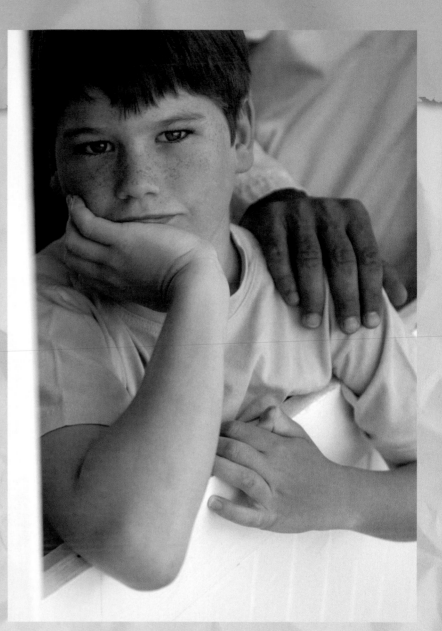

When Jake's father died, his mother took it badly. She was very ill and was losing weight, and the grief of losing her husband caused her to lose more weight. Jake was worried about his mother during this time. He had been attending church with his aunt and he decided to confide in a local pastor. The pastor was sympathetic and he came to the house to pray with his mother, which seemed to comfort her. This made Jake feel much better because he felt he was actually doing something to help his mother.

Jake didn't go to either of his parents' funerals. He had wanted to attend his mother's funeral but it was decided that he shouldn't go, although he can't remember who made this decision. Jake stayed with a relative and can't remember much about that day – it all seems like a bad dream. Losing his mother affected him very

▲ Jake is now happy with his aunt and uncle, but he still misses his mum and dad. AIDS orphans often experience distress and social isolation and this can lead to shame, fear and loneliness. Jake receives lots of support from his aunt and uncle and they have helped him come to terms with his situation.

badly – he felt as if his whole world had fallen apart and it was a long time before he started to feel he could enjoy life again.

Jake is amazed how some people react when he tells them how his parents died. Many people still believe that Jake must be infected if both his parents were HIV+. It is difficult to deal with such prejudice and Jake finds their comments hurtful. He would like

How HIV/AIDS is not passed on

Those who are HIV+ would find life a lot easier if people realized the many ways that the disease *cannot* be passed on. As Jake is well aware, it is not passed on through normal social contact such as sharing cups, plates or cutlery with an infected person. It also cannot be passed on by sharing a toilet seat or bath, or by touching or kissing someone with HIV or AIDS if you both have healthy, unbroken skin. Neither can you become infected just by living and caring for someone with the condition.

everyone to be made aware about HIV/AIDS so that they understand how the disease can and can't be passed on. Jake thinks it's important for young people to be educated about HIV/AIDS at school. He feels this would have helped him cope a little better.

Jake now lives with his aunt and uncle just a short way from his old house. He is very glad they adopted him because it meant he didn't have to change schools. Although he still misses his mother and father very much, Jake knows his aunt and uncle love him, and he is positive about the future.

► Diana, Princess of Wales, did much to publicize HIV and AIDS. She was often pictured touching and holding AIDS victims, and this helped change people's attitudes to the disease. Here we see her carrying an HIV+ girl during a visit to a care home in Washington, DC. Those who are HIV+ would find life a lot easier if people realized the many ways that the disease cannot be passed on. As Jake is well aware, it is not passed on through normal social contact such as holding hands.

Coco's Story
France

Coco is 14 and lives in Paris with her father, stepmother and two younger brothers. She attends a school just outside the centre of Paris and does all the normal things any teenage girl does. But Coco is not like any teenage girl – she was born with HIV, which she contracted from her mother who was an intravenous drug user. Coco's mother died when Coco was a baby. Her father remarried and she now has two half-brothers aged nine and six.

Coco is a confident girl and deals with her condition in a very mature way. When she was younger, people used to make fun of her, which she found very upsetting. Now she is better able to deal with cruel comments. Coco isn't afraid to be upfront about her condition and she made sure her friends were aware that she was HIV+.

'When I told by friends in high school, they were really supportive. My best friend cried when I told her – she hugged me and said she still loved me. I have been lucky because, apart from a few people at my old school who made cruel comments, everyone else has supported me.'

Coco's father told her about her mother and HIV when she was very young. 'He wanted me to realize that I had done nothing wrong – it's just a condition like any other. And I am still Coco, whether I am HIV+ or not. If people don't want to be my friend just because I have HIV, then I don't want their friendship anyway!'

Coco is lucky to have a supportive network of friends and family. However, she has been through some tough times. In her previous school a group of girls bullied her because she is HIV+. 'They used to pick on me and tell others not to touch me, which

Dating

Dating can be tricky with HIV. At first Coco didn't want to tell any potential boyfriends that she was HIV+. She went out with her first boyfriend for three months before telling him. He broke up with her straight away and Coco found it difficult to deal with the rejection. Her stepmother explained that it was best to be open from the start so there was no danger of any misunderstanding. It was important to be honest if she wanted to have a close relationship with a boy.

really hurt. My dad told me to ignore them because they didn't understand about HIV. My school dealt with it but the bullying didn't stop, although it wasn't as bad. Now I am at a different school and my friends all stick up for me!'

▼ **Coco realizes that she needs to be honest with potential boyfriends and tell them she is HIV+ as soon as possible. 'I don't want them to think I want to keep my condition a secret,' she explains. 'It's only fair to tell them so they can decide what to do.'**

Wayne's Story
United Kingdom

At a college in West London, Wayne is about to start an apprenticeship in carpentry. He is looking forward to receiving on-the-job training and working towards a qualification. However, things weren't always looking so positive for Wayne. His father contracted HIV and hepatitis C from a former partner in the 1980s. As a young child, Wayne watched as his father had to go in and out of hospital, growing weaker all the time. Sadly, his father died of cancer when Wayne was seven.

Children orphaned by HIV/AIDS

Around the world, more than 15 million children under 18 have been orphaned due to HIV/AIDS. Children whose parents are sick with HIV may suffer neglect long before they become orphans. If their parents die, they must adjust to a new situation with little or no support, and may suffer stigma within their communities, leading to psychological problems. They may also suffer lack of access to basic necessities such as food, clothing, health care and education. Orphaned siblings may be split up so as not to overburden foster families. This can be another upsetting experience for them to deal with.

Wayne's mother left them when Wayne was three and his sister Clare was nine, leaving his sick father to care for them. Wayne can't remember much about this time because he was so young. But he does remember his father's regular trips to the doctor or hospital, and the amount of medication he had to take as his illness progressed. He also remembers the endless colds and coughs his father had, and the time he had to ring the emergency services because his father was having difficulty breathing.

When Wayne was five, he and Clare were placed in a children's care home. His father could no longer care for them due to his illness, although they visited him regularly at home and when he was in hospital. His father spent the last four weeks of his life in a hospice. Wayne remembers the last time he went with Clare to see him. He was very weak but he managed to hold their hands before saying goodbye. It was a very upsetting experience, but Wayne is glad he said goodbye to his father.

After their father's death, Wayne and Clare were placed in separate foster homes. This was the first time they had been apart and Wayne missed his sister very much. By this time Clare was 13, but she still found the situation difficult to deal with. As the years passed, Wayne lost contact with his sister.

◄ **Wayne found it difficult to cope with losing both his parents and he was often in trouble at school. Children who have lost their parents to AIDS are frequently assumed to be HIV+ themselves, making them more likely to suffer discrimination. It has taken Wayne a long time to come to terms with his anger, but his foster parents have been very supportive and have helped him all they can.**

Back in the 1980s, little was known about HIV/AIDS. As a result, Wayne's father's diagnosis came too late and the condition had already reached a critical stage by the time he started receiving treatment. Since then, medical science has made some impressive breakthroughs in the battle against HIV/AIDS.

Wayne has been with his current foster parents for three years and he is about to move away and find his own accommodation near his college in London. Wayne hasn't always wanted to study. He didn't like school and found it difficult to concentrate. He was always getting into trouble and was excluded from three schools.

When he was excluded from his last school, his foster parents arranged for him to receive tuition at home. They have always been

Advances in the treatment of HIV/AIDS

In the early 1980s when HIV/AIDS were first detected, people with the condition could not expect to live longer than a few years. In 1987 the first antiretroviral drug (ARV) was approved to treat the disease. Called AZT, it prevented the virus from copying itself in the cells. In 1996 a treatment known as HAART (highly active antiretroviral therapy), which uses a combination of ARVs, became available. This has proved far more effective than taking individual ARVs. Today there are more than 30 ARVs, giving patients a wide choice of treatments. Although ARVs do not cure HIV/AIDS, they suppress the virus so that people infected with HIV can live longer, healthier lives. The ARVs do not completely eliminate HIV from the body, and people who are HIV+ can still transmit the virus. They must take ARVs for the rest of their life.

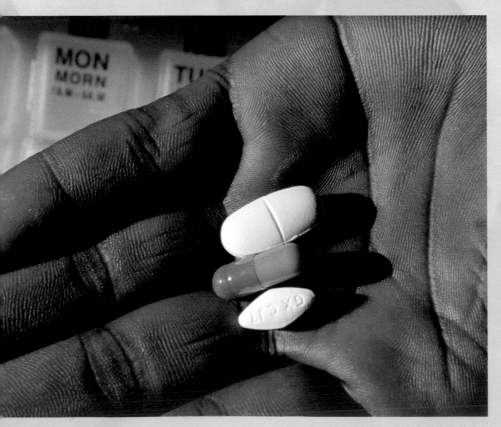

◄ As an HIV+ patient in South Africa, Bavuyise Mbebe must take three different ARV drugs each day to help increase his white blood cell count. People with HIV should start ARV treatment when their count dips below 200. At one point Bavuyise's count fell to 184. He is one of the lucky ones. A year's supply of ARV drugs costs around $12,000 (£7,700) – too expensive for most HIV patients. However, his treatment is provided by the Siyaphila La (We are living here) programme.

▲ **Wayne had to learn how to deal with his anger and rejection. He enjoys working with his hands and he realizes that if he works hard and gains qualifications in carpentry, it will help him find a job. He has made new friends at college and now feels more able to talk about his feelings. He plans to try and contact his sister when he has finished his course, and he remains positive about the future.**

very supportive and they encouraged him to enrol on a carpentry apprenticeship because he enjoys working with his hands. Wayne is grateful to them because they stood by him through some very difficult times. He doesn't believe he would be in college now if it wasn't for their love and patience.

Wayne is still dealing with a lot of anger. He is angry about his mother's rejection and that his father died before he could benefit from modern ARVs and HAART. He is also angry that he was parted from his sister. Most of all, he is angry that HIV/AIDS robbed him of his father when he was so young. However, Wayne knows he needs to deal with these issues and let go of his anger so that he can move forward. His foster parents and the tutors at his new college have given him the support he needs to develop, as well as an opportunity to make a new life for himself.

Ebenezer's Story
South Africa

Angie has lost her husband, four children and three grandchildren to AIDS. Her only surviving grandchild is 16-year-old Ebenezer, who lives with her in the Western Cape. Ebenezer is HIV+. His mother – Angie's daughter – died three years ago, leaving Angie to look after him. Ebenezer's mother, Suni, was infected by her husband, Jules. The younger children were infected at birth or through breastfeeding. Ebenezer was not infected by his mother but by having unprotected sex. He is very sick and Angie does her best to care for him.

In South Africa, around 5.2 million people live with HIV – more than in any other country. About one in nine of the country's population are infected with the virus. In parts of South Africa, children become sexually active at an early age, which increases the spread of HIV among children, particularly if condoms are not used. In sub-Saharan Africa 16 per cent of young women (aged 15–19) and 12 per cent of young men report having sex before they were 15. Ebenezer was infected by one of his sexual partners and Angie is very sad because she thought he was the only grandchild to have escaped the disease.

Ebenezer's father, Jules, left home when Ebenezer was a baby, and his mother, Suni, married again. Suni didn't know that Jules was HIV+. Jules had become infected when he spent two years in prison. Suni had three more children with Jules. She and the children all contracted HIV.

When Ebenezer first became ill, he thought he had a cold or flu. His skin felt dry and flaky and started to peel. He had a sore throat that wouldn't get better and his neck was swollen. He then began to have difficulty sleeping and felt exhausted all the time. His grandmother managed to pay for him to visit a doctor. The doctor took one look inside his mouth and diagnosed a tumour. He arranged for Ebenezer to have blood tests for HIV that came back positive. Ebenezer was shocked.

▶ Ten-year-old HIV+ orphan Zamo Mdingwe fetches water outside his village of Xurana, South Africa. Zamo lost his mother to AIDS four years ago and he started taking ARV treatment a year later. He is now healthy and living the life of a normal child. Without the ARV drugs he would probably be dead by now. Children in poor countries must work hard to help their families by doing chores around the house, and the loss of a parent to AIDS can seriously affect a child's access to shelter, food, clothing, health and education.

HIV/AIDS in South African prisons

Approximately 41 per cent of the inmates in South Africa's prisons are HIV+. Many arrive in prison already HIV+. They pass the disease on through unprotected sex with other inmates or by sharing needles used to inject themselves with drugs. South African prisons are very overcrowded, so prisoners are often left unsupervised, increasing the risk of gang activity and sexual violence. Youths are often incarcerated alongside adult prisoners. All of these things contribute to the spread of HIV/AIDS in South African prisons.

The medication Ebenezer needs is not always easy to get hold of. He needs to take four different ARVs to boost his immune system and suppress the virus in his blood. He must travel every month to a medical centre 29 kilometres away, which is run by a local AIDS charity. It provides him with the drugs he needs, but the centre is threatened with closure unless it receives more funding. If it closes, the nearest centre that provides free ARVs will be 117 kilometres from Ebenezer's home town.

Ebenezer struggles to earn enough money to buy food for himself and his grandmother. He grows dates and figs on a small patch of land at the front of his tiny house and sells them along the side of the road. He has started to grow soybeans to try to make some extra money and he is saving up to buy another plot of land at the back of his house. He would like to go to school but he has no choice but to work.

Ebenezer is bitter about the loss of his family. He would like more to be done to help his country deal with HIV/AIDS. He knows that it is only through ignorance that the disease spreads. He wants to do all he can to warn people: 'I was stupid and didn't protect myself. Unprotected sex is one of the most common ways of getting HIV. I had a chance to stay healthy – to look after my grandmother – but I've thrown it all away. Now I am HIV+ and sometimes my grandmother needs to take care of me. I need to take medication every day, but I can't always get the medicine I need because of the cost.'

▶ Zamo carries his bag of ARV medicine into his house. The drugs were provided by the Siyaphila La (We are living here) programme, which is making ARV treatment available in poor, rural districts. The ARVs reduce the concentration of HIV circulating in the blood. As with all drugs, ARVs have side effects, such as stomach pain, nausea and diarrhoea. Forgetting to take the medication can quickly lead to drug resistance, which means the drugs no longer work. Scientists continue to research new ways of treating HIV/AIDS.

▲ AIDS campaigners in South Africa celebrate World AIDS Day. The day has been observed on 1 December each year since 1988 as a means of raising public awareness of the disease. These campaigners are all HIV+ and are members of the organization TAC (Treatment Action Campaign), which fights to make HIV testing and treatment available to all who need it.

Educating people about HIV/AIDS

AIDS charities and government departments have been running a number of campaigns in South Africa to raise awareness of the disease. Khomanani, meaning 'caring together', has been going since 2001, using TV and radio to try to spread its message to as many people as possible. The campaign loveLife, running since 1999, is aimed particularly at teens. It has youth centres around the country that also offer clinics and counselling. In a 2008 survey it was found that more than four-fifths of South Africans had seen or heard at least one HIV/AIDS campaign and that 15–24 year olds were the most receptive. Despite this, there remains widespread ignorance about the causes of HIV transmission with less than half the population aware that safe sex and fewer partners lowered the risk of infection.

The future for Ebenezer is uncertain as he waits to find out whether the local medical centre will stay open. While he is taking the ARVs he is able to keep the condition under control, but he still has days when he feels too tired to work. He hopes to go back to college one day to get the education he missed out on. For now, he takes each day as it comes and tries to keep a positive outlook.

Mala's Story
Zambia

During her short life, 15-year-old Mala has faced some tough challenges. As a little girl she was very happy, living with her parents in Sesheke in south-western Zambia. She was doing well at school and dreamed of being a lawyer one day. But her world fell apart when she lost both her parents to HIV/AIDS. She was only nine years old.

After her parents died, Mala went to stay with an aunt, Neti, who inherited Mala's parents' property. Neti promised to send Mala to a good school, and Mala thought things would carry on as before. She was looking forward to going back to school with her old friends, but Neti had other ideas. She refused to pay for Mala's education. Instead she made her work in the house, cooking, cleaning and caring for Neti's three small children.

Life with Neti was very harsh. She beat Mala if she did not do her chores and Neti's husband often joined in with the beatings. Even though Mala wasn't much older than her cousins, she had to cook and clean for them and do their laundry while they went to school. 'I felt so bad every day – I didn't want to get out of bed in the morning because I knew I would be beaten. I missed my mother so much and I used to cry myself to sleep every night.'

AIDS orphans in Zambia

HIV/AIDS has had a devastating effect on Zambia. An estimated 19 per cent of children under 18, or 1.1 million, are orphans — most due to HIV/AIDS. Many households are now headed by children as young as 11. In other cases, children must take care of sick parents and some are forced to leave school to care for family members. There is very little support for children affected by HIV/AIDS and a severe lack of foster homes to care for them. Many are abandoned due to social stigma or lack of resources. Others run away from foster homes because they have been mistreated or abused by foster families, and end up homeless on the streets.

When she was 12, Mala ran away to Lusaka, the capital of Zambia. She had nowhere to go and to earn money she turned to prostitution. A year later she fell pregnant. When her daughter was born, Mala was just 14. She and her child lived rough on the streets until she was spotted by a charity worker. He arranged for Mala to move to a hostel where she receives food and shelter as well as a basic education. Mala is one of the lucky ones — there are thousands of orphans on the streets of Zambia who aren't given this opportunity.

▶ **(Opposite) There are millions of children like Mala who have been orphaned by AIDS. This 15-year-old orphaned girl in Mwaiseni, Zambia, has a two-year-old daughter to support. As well as the lack of education, AIDS orphans also miss out on valuable life skills and practical knowledge that would have been passed on to them by their parents.**

Claudia's Story
Honduras

Claudia is 11 and lives in Tocoa in northern Honduras. Her mother Rosa contracted HIV from Claudia's father, who died a year ago. Claudia's younger sister was born with HIV and died aged six months. Claudia watches her mother grow weaker every day. She shares the job of caring for her with Gina, Rosa's closest friend, who is also HIV+. Gina does her best to care for Rosa and Claudia, but her own health isn't good.

Children with HIV+ parents

In many families children become the main carers for people who are ill with HIV or AIDS. Older children must often play the parenting role for their younger siblings. In some cases, children as young as eight have to take on the responsibility of caring for the family and earning a living. As a result, many children miss out on schooling. They must cope daily with the fear that their parents will die and the uncertainty of what will become of them.

Rosa first realized she was HIV+ when Claudia's little sister died. The baby was only six months old and very sick – she wouldn't stop crying and wouldn't eat and Rosa knew there was something seriously wrong with her. Rosa had a blood test, and it confirmed her worst fears. Rosa thinks her husband must have caught HIV from prostitutes and then infected her with the virus. Prostitution is responsible for a great deal of the spread of HIV within communities because one prostitute can infect many people.

For Claudia, life as a young carer can be frustrating. 'Gina has been helping me,' she explains, 'but Gina has HIV, too, and sometimes she has bad days so I don't manage to get to school because they both need me.' Claudia's story is very common. Around the world, children are being forced to leave school to care for parents who are HIV+ or who have full-blown AIDS.

Claudia is only a child, but she must take on the responsibilities of an adult. 'I don't mind caring for my mother,' she says. 'But sometimes I wish I could go to school regularly like other children. Sometimes Gina can stay with my mother and then I get to go out. But other times Gina feels too sick so I have to care for them both.'

Rosa and Gina need to take medication for their illness every day. They are lucky – they receive their ARVs from a local medical centre, which is sponsored by an AIDS charity. Rosa and Gina are aware of the pressure that Claudia is under. Rosa would like her to go to school, but needs her to help in the house sometimes.

◀ **Rosa and Claudia listen as the doctor confirms that Rosa is HIV+. Claudia did not fully understand what it meant when she learned that her mother had the disease, but she soon realized that her carefree childhood was over. She has had to miss out on school and often doesn't have time to play with her friends – something most young people take for granted.**

Claudia has been tested for HIV and thankfully the test came back negative. Tests for HIV involve taking blood from the arm or from a pinprick on the finger. Signs of infection don't show up immediately but take a few weeks to develop. For most people, the first signs of infection will show up in their blood within two months of contracting the disease.

▼ **Claudia is tested for HIV. Everyone was relieved when the test turned out to be negative. When a person has HIV, their immune system produces antibodies to fight the infection. The appearance of these antibodies in the blood shows that a person is HIV+.**

How to prevent the spread of HIV

The risk of of HIV infection can be reduced in the following ways:

- People should abstain from sex or delay first sex, be faithful to one partner or have fewer partners; if they have sex, they should always use a condom.

- Drug addicts should avoid sharing equipment, including needles, to inject drugs.

- All blood supplies and blood products should be screened for the virus.

- Equipment used for tattooing and circumcision should be sterilized.

- ARV drugs should be given to HIV+ mothers during pregnancy and labour and to their newborn babies.

- HIV+ mothers should not breastfeed when safe replacements are available.

▶ **Rosa prepares herself a healthy dish. For HIV+ patients, good nutrition helps to maintain a strong immune system. They should eat plenty of fresh fruit and vegetables, as well as meat, fish and eggs. A healthy diet not only helps them to fight infection, but also enables them to respond to ARVs more effectively.**

The blood of all infected people will show signs within three months. Therefore if someone is tested soon after they think they were infected and the result is negative, it is best if they go back for another test three months later to make sure they are really free of the virus.

Things are looking brighter for Claudia. Gina is getting stronger and Rosa is responding well to treatment. The two women have started earning a living by doing laundry and clothing repairs for wealthier families. With the extra money they have bought more fruit and vegetables, because a healthy diet is extremely important when a person is HIV+. It helps build up the immune system so that the body can fight off infections.

Because their health has improved, Rosa thinks that Claudia can go back to school full-time very soon. Claudia knows she will have to work hard to catch up on all the studies she has missed, but she is looking forward to seeing her classmates again and she is delighted to see her mother and Gina looking so much better.

Matthew's Story
United States

Matthew is a lively 13-year-old from New Jersey. He was born with HIV. Nobody knew he had the disease until he started showing symptoms when he was 12. His fingernails started to fall off, his skin became dry and flaky, he felt tired all the time and became breathless very easily. His doctor arranged for blood tests. When it was discovered that Matthew was HIV+, the doctor realized he must have been infected at birth. His mother had died of AIDS-related cancer the previous year and it was following her death that Matthew had started showing symptoms.

Matthew now lives with his aunt and her partner. Matthew is lucky because he started receiving treatment before the virus had done too much damage to his immune system. Since one ARV isn't strong enough to fight HIV alone, he takes a large number of different ARV drugs every day.

Matthew knows that he cannot miss a dose because this can result in the virus becoming resistant to the medication and it won't work as well. Matthew is determined never to miss a dose. He realizes there is currently no cure for HIV. Drugs can extend his life and improve his general health, but cannot rid his body of the virus. Yet he is hopeful of a medical breakthrough in the future.

Since he started to take his medication, Matthew's health has improved. His nails have grown back, his skin is no longer so dry and he has more energy than before. Things are also going well at school. His teachers have been extremely supportive throughout the past year and he has had extra tuition to help him catch up on the schooling he missed when he was ill.

Matthew is still getting over the loss of his mother – he misses her tremendously and certainly doesn't blame her for his condition. He believes it is important to educate young people about HIV/AIDS, because there are still many myths surrounding the condition.

▶ **Matthew receives extra tuition for the schooling he's missed while he was in hospital. Without a good school education, children are more likely to face social, economic and health problems as they grow up. Matthew is fortunate that his school has systems in place to make sure he catches up on all the schoolwork he missed.**

Ignorance about HIV/AIDS

In the United States, young people are becoming sexually active at an earlier age — sometimes as young as 11 years old. According to research, around 10 per cent of 12 year olds and 40 per cent of 16 year olds are sexually active. Although 15 per cent of high school students admitted to having had four or more sexual partners, many do not use condoms. One in four sexually active teenagers contracts a sexually transmitted disease, yet surveys have shown that more than 50 per cent of teenagers believe they are not at risk of getting HIV and, even if they did, they believed it would not develop into AIDS. However, nearly half of all new HIV infections occur in people under 25 years old, and most are infected through sex.

When Matthew discovered he was HIV+, he found it difficult to tell his friends. At first he kept his condition secret, but eventually he confided in a teacher at school. She was very supportive and gave Matthew a number of booklets about HIV and how to cope with it.

One morning, when he arrived a school, a group of boys stopped him in the playground and asked: 'Is it true you've got AIDS?' Matthew was shocked and didn't know what to say. He spoke to the teacher who had helped him and she told him she hadn't mentioned it to anyone. Matthew suspects that someone saw him reading the HIV booklet and put two and two together.

All of Matthew's classmates are now aware that he is HIV+. Because Matthew feels so strongly about educating people, he decided to write an

▲ Young people who are HIV+ can find it difficult to tell their friends and classmates about their condition. Some young people, like Matthew, have been bullied because they are HIV+. It is important for them to find someone they trust, such as a parent or teacher, in whom they can confide. They can then discuss their plans for the future and look at ways to construct their lives positively.

article about his illness for his school magazine. Most of the students at his school have made positive comments, but there are a few that persist in name-calling.

He has also received some hateful text messages and emails, but he shrugs them off: 'I was called things like "mud blood" and "bad blood" and those kind of things. Most people don't know anything about HIV. I think it's my job to let them know what it is. I didn't do anything wrong, I was born with this virus – I'm not unclean or anything. People say bad things because they're ignorant and don't know what they're talking about. I have a chance to let people know exactly what HIV is and how to protect themselves from it.'

Since his article appeared in the school magazine, Matthew has been contacted by his local newspaper and asked to write an article for it. He sees this as an excellent opportunity to educate his peers about HIV. It also gives him the chance to explain how HIV has affected his life.

Matthew is considering a career in journalism and is studying hard to improve his grades. He thinks that journalism will give him a platform to speak out about the stigma that is still attached to people with HIV, and the discrimination they face. Also, if young people know the facts about HIV, they are more likely to take steps to protect themselves and stop the virus from spreading.

HIV/AIDS and young people

Young people in their late teens and early 20s are the category most at risk of contracting HIV/AIDS. Today, 45 per cent of all new cases of HIV worldwide are aged between 15 and 24. There are 11.8 million HIV+ young people around the world, of which more than 7 million are female. The main problem remains ignorance. Less than one-third of young people worldwide know how to protect themselves from HIV. For this reason, many governments and campaigning organizations have launched programmes to encourage condom use, delaying first sex, faithfulness to a single partner and early HIV testing and treatment.

▲ When Matthew was given the opportunity to write about HIV for his school magazine, he realized that this was an opportunity to educate people. He wants to train to be a journalist when he leaves school because he sees this as a way of informing people about HIV/AIDS and helping to remove the stigma attached to the disease.

JD's Story
United States

JD is a 16-year-old African-American girl serving three months in a New York detention centre for juvenile offenders. She was originally convicted for delivering street drugs over nine months ago and has been in youth detention twice since then. JD contracted HIV while in detention through sharing needles. Sadly, she is one of a growing number of HIV+ youths living in detention centres.

JD's mother abandoned her when she was seven. After that, she went to stay with her aunt. Although her aunt worked long hours, she couldn't afford to buy JD the clothes or shoes JD wanted. To earn some extra money, JD started delivering street drugs for the neighbourhood dealers. Soon she started taking drugs herself. To pay for her addiction to drugs, she did drug deliveries rather than go to school. Because of this, she missed out on much of her education.

At the youth detention centre, nights are generally unsupervised and fights often break out between the inmates. JD has had to learn to stick up for herself because there is still a stigma attached to being HIV+. She has been verbally and physically abused and has even received death threats.

◄ Having been abandoned by her mother as a child, JD spent much of her time on the streets as a drug runner. Despite the efforts of her aunt and uncle, she ended up in a detention centre. Here she contracted HIV through sharing needles with other drug users. JD is now determined to stay off drugs for good.

▲ Drug users who share needles put themselves at risk of getting HIV. JD found this out the hard way and is now dealing with the consequences.

JD is now more determined than ever to learn from her past. 'I'm not coming back in here ever again. I've had it with detention and their rules and regulations. This isn't a life – I know I can do better than this. I've messed up big time but I need to cut it and move on. I get out of here in six weeks and I need to make sure I get treatment for my condition and do something with my life.'

HIV/AIDS and drug use

Sharing syringes and other equipment for drug injection is one means by which the HIV virus can spread. But it is not just drug users who are at risk. People who have sex with an injection drug user (IDU) risk infection, as do children born to mothers who are IDUs or who have had sex with IDUs. Since HIV/AIDS first emerged, injection drug use has directly or indirectly accounted for 36 per cent of AIDS cases in the United States. IDU-associated AIDS more commonly affects women than men.

JD will move back in with her aunt when she is released from detention. It won't be easy living back in that neighbourhood with the same old temptations. JD wants to get help for her drug addiction – and not only for herself. She knows that using drugs could impair her judgement and lead her to have unprotected sex, thereby transmitting the disease to someone else.

At the end of her three-month sentence, JD was released from detention and moved back in with her aunt, who lives just a few blocks from her old drug-dealing contacts. She knows she must stay away from these places if she wants her health to improve. She has taken a greater interest in her health and the treatment she is receiving for the HIV.

'I take a whole cocktail of drugs now – all sorts of things – but they aren't the type of drugs I used to take. These ones are to help my immune system. I know I probably need to take these for the rest of my life. Because I couldn't afford to pay for my medication, I was able to get them through the AIDS Drug Assistance Program. If it wasn't for this programme, I don't know what I'd do.'

When JD was asked what could be done to help young people in youth detention centres who were HIV+ or who had AIDS, she said: 'They need to have confidential blood tests done on everyone in detention centres. Some people could be infected but not realize it, and this would help prevent it spreading around. We also need counselling because I was devastated when I found out I was HIV+. I would have found it helpful to talk to someone. I didn't even understand what HIV was and I had nobody to ask.'

The AIDS Drug Assistance Program has been a great support for JD. She has been put in touch with a counsellor who meets JD every two weeks. They discuss everything, including HIV/AIDS, relationships, drug addiction and dealing with discrimination. JD's aunt has also been very supportive and has attended a number of HIV information sessions with JD, which has helped her understand what she can do to help. It hasn't been easy for JD since leaving the detention centre. There are many temptations around her and it would be easy to go back to her old ways. But as JD said: 'I'm not going back in there ever again!'

Help for the disadvantaged

HIV/AIDS is more prevalent among the poorer sections of society, who are also the least able to afford the necessary treatment. In the United States, most people have private medical insurance to cover the cost of their health care. However, poorer people are either underinsured or lack insurance altogether. HIV medication is expensive. It costs approximately $500 (£321) per month for the most expensive HIV drugs and around $15,000 (£9,600) a year for all the drugs required to control the condition. To help those who can't afford to pay for their medication, a programme called the Ryan White Care Act was set up in 1990. This provides federal funds for the treatment of low-income victims of HIV/AIDS. Around 500,000 Americans are helped each year by this programme. About one-third of the funds go to the AIDS Drug Assistance Program, which has been providing JD with treatment.

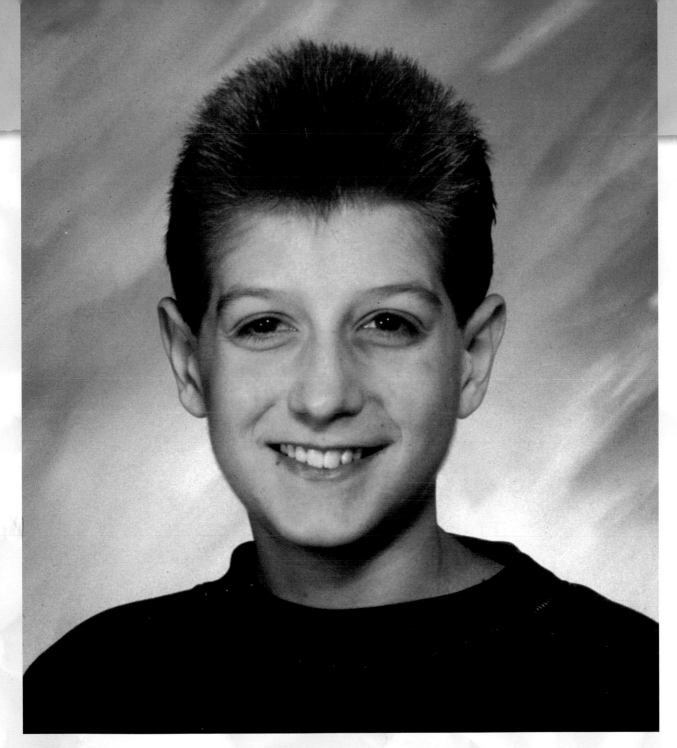

▲ This is Ryan White, who inspired the Ryan White Care Act (see panel opposite). Ryan was born in 1971 with haemophilia and he accidentally contracted HIV during medical treatment. He was excluded from his school in Kokomo, Indiana, because parents and teachers wrongly believed he would infect other children. Ryan's family fought the decision through the courts and the case made national headlines. Due to pressure from his school and threats of violence, Ryan and his family moved to Cicero, Indiana. The trial, however, made Ryan famous. When he died in 1990, following a lung infection, Elton John sang at his funeral. During his short life, Ryan did much to change people's attitudes towards HIV/AIDS and after his death many charities were set up to increase awareness of the disease and to provide support for victims of HIV and their families.

Manu's Story
Australia

Manu spends much of his time in his bedroom playing his guitar, dreaming of joining a band and becoming a rock star. He seems like any other 14-year-old boy, and he is – except Manu has had to deal with a lot more heartache than most other kids of his age. Manu was born with HIV, which he contracted from his mother. She had caught it from Manu's father. Manu never knew his father, who abandoned the family when Manu was six months old. His mother died when he was six. Since then he's been living with foster parents in Adelaide.

Manu is surprisingly relaxed about his illness. He has been affected by HIV and AIDS all his life, so it doesn't feel unusual to him. He can't recall much about his mother, although he has a scrapbook full of photographs and birthday and Christmas cards from her. The virus took her from him, but it hasn't made him bitter.

Occasionally he gets angry about his illness – but then he remembers that he is one of the lucky ones. 'I read about other people around the world with HIV. Some people can't get the medication they need. I'm lucky – at least I am taken care of and, as long as I take my medication, I feel okay.'

▶ It can be hard for a young person with HIV living in foster care, but Manu remains positive. He loves to play his guitar and has even started to write his own songs. He realizes that he needs to be strong in order to overcome prejudice, and that this prejudice stems from fear and misinformation. He plans to use his musical abilities to tackle this ignorance about HIV/AIDS.

▲ Manu finds it is better to tell girlfriends about his condition as early as possible rather than risk them finding out from someone else. It is a difficult issue to discuss and Manu isn't always sure how a girl will react, but he thinks it is better to be honest right at the beginning before things get serious.

Manu hopes he will not be in foster care for much longer, but he realizes that as he gets older, the chances of being adopted by a family become slimmer. 'It's a bit unfair,' he says. 'I always hoped to find a family that wanted me to be their son. I know that it probably won't happen now because I have HIV and no one wants to adopt me.'

Manu enjoys school and he has had girlfriends. 'I don't tell everyone I am HIV+. But if I want to ask a girl out, I think it's only fair to tell her about my HIV. Sometimes girls back off and treat me like I have the plague, but I've had a couple of really nice girlfriends, so you never know!'

How to tell others you are HIV+

Before telling others you have HIV, think about the following:

- Why do you want to tell people? How do you think they will react?

- Be prepared. Learn as much as you can about HIV. Have some educational material to hand, including leaflets and brochures.

- Discuss your plans with someone you trust who knows you have HIV. Ask your doctor to write a short letter for you to give to people.

- Let them deal with the news in their own way. Give them time to digest the information.

Lian's Story
Singapore

Lian has lived with her grandparents in Singapore for most of her life. She doesn't remember her mother, who died from AIDS-related cancer when she was 18 months old. At around the same time, Lian was diagnosed as being HIV+. Although AIDS is not as widespread in Singapore as it is in some neighbouring countries, the rate at which new cases are appearing is on the increase. Luckily Lian's infection was detected early, and so the treatment has been effective. She is now 15 years old and is a promising student.

Because she has grown up with HIV, Lian is not worried about telling people she is HIV+. However, some of the neighbours in the close-knit community where she lives did not always treat her kindly. Whenever her grandparents took her to the clinic, a few neighbours waited outside her house when she returned. They used to point and stare and shout things at her. This made her grandparents very angry. They called the police a few times and eventually the harassment stopped.

Stigma and discrimination

As Lian discovered, few diseases arouse as much hostility towards its victims as HIV/AIDS. There are several reasons for this. Firstly, it is a contagious disease, and people are naturally frightened of becoming infected. Secondly, HIV/AIDS is associated with behaviour that many find distasteful, such as sexual promiscuity and drug use. Thirdly, HIV/AIDS is a relatively new disease and there is a great deal of ignorance about its causes. This has allowed myths to arise, which have added to people's prejudices. People with HIV face the double challenge of dealing with their illness as well as the stigma that surrounds it. Education is the only way of overcoming this stigma. If people become better acquainted with the facts about HIV/AIDS, they are more likely to behave sympathetically towards its victims.

Lian is a very good student and hopes to study mathematics at university when she is older. She is also very interested in science and has won many school awards. Last year her school entered a science contest with all the local schools. Lian helped her school win first prize. Lian's grandparents are very proud of her achievements and are pleased she has not allowed HIV to ruin her life.

When Lian turned 15, she went to a school dance and was asked out by a boy for the first time. She had discussed HIV with her family and close friends many times, but she didn't feel comfortable talking about HIV to a stranger, especially a boy. At first

$2 \times 2x = 10$

$4x = 10$

$5x = 10$

$x = \dfrac{10}{5}$

$x = 2$

▲ **Lian is determined not to let the fact that she is HIV+ stop her from doing what she wants to do. She loves mathematics and science and intends to study mathematics at university. By making a success of her life, she hopes she will be able to change people's attitudes towards HIV/AIDS.**

she wasn't sure what to do, but finally she decided to be upfront and told him she was HIV+. She expected him to make his excuses and leave, but surprisingly he didn't and nearly a year later, they are still going out together.

Glossary

abstinence Restraint from indulging in something, such as sex.

AIDS (Acquired immunodeficiency syndrome) A disease of the human immune system caused by the human immunodeficiency virus (HIV).

ARVs (Antiretroviral drugs) Medications for the treatment of HIV. They have this name because HIV is a type of virus called a retrovirus.

AZT A drug used in the past to delay the development of AIDS in HIV+ patients.

bodily fluids Liquids that are inside the bodies of animals. They include blood, semen, vaginal fluid and breast milk.

caesarean section An operation to deliver a baby by cutting through a mother's abdomen and womb.

cancer A malignant growth or tumour caused by abnormal cell division, which can spread to other parts of the body.

circumcision The removal of the foreskin from the penis.

condom A close-fitting rubber covering worn by a man over the penis during sexual intercourse. It is used to prevent pregnancy or the spread of sexually transmitted diseases.

contract Catch or develop a disease.

detention centre A centre where convicted offenders are held in custody.

diagnosis The identification of the nature or cause of an illness or infection.

discrimination Unfair treatment of one person or group because they differ in some way from the majority of people.

HAART (Highly active antiretroviral therapy) A treatment for HIV that involves taking a combination (usually three or four) ARV drugs.

haemophilia A condition in which the ability of the blood to clot is reduced, causing sufferers to bleed severely from the slightest injury.

hepatitis C An inflammation of the liver, causing fever, abdominal pain and weakness.

HIV (Human immunodeficiency virus) A disease that causes the immune system to fail, leading to AIDS.

hospice A home for terminally ill patients.

immune system A system of cells, tissues and organs that defend the body against attacks from disease-causing microorganisms.

incarcerate Put someone in prison.

incubation The development of an infection inside the body to the point at which the first signs of the disease become apparent.

lymph nodes Oval organs that form part of the lymphatic system. They are found under the arms, and in the groin, neck and abdomen. They act as filters for the lymph fluid.

pneumonia An inflammation of the lungs caused by viruses, bacteria or other microorganisms.

prejudice An opinion about something that is based on insufficient knowledge or irrational feelings.

safe sex Sexual activity in which precautions are taken to avoid spreading sexually transmitted diseases, for example by wearing a condom.

screening Testing someone to see if they have an illness.

stigma The shame or disgrace attached to something regarded as socially unacceptable.

sub-Saharan Africa The region of Africa to the south of the Sahara Desert.

suppress Put an end to the effects of something, such as a virus.

symptom An indication of a particular disease, especially one experienced by the patient.

transfusion The transfer of blood from a healthy donor to someone who is sick.

transmission The act or process of transmitting, or spreading, something, such as a disease.

tumour A swelling formed by an abnormal growth of cells.

virus An infectious organism that replicates itself only within the cells of living hosts.

Further Information

Books

Be a Friend: Children Who Live With HIV Speak by Aprille Best, Philip Pizzo and Lori Wiener (Albert Whitman & Company, 1999)

Essential Issues: HIV/AIDS by Katie Marsico (Abdo Publishing, 2010)

HIV Positive by Bernard Wolf (Dutton Juvenile, 1997)

A Name on the Quilt: A Story of Remembrance by Jeannine Atkins (Aladdin, 2003)

Watch Out, He's Got AIDS: A Story for Kids and Parents by Mikey Handis (Water Row Press, 1998)

What If We Do Nothing? AIDS and Other Epidemics by Carol Ballard (Franklin Watts, 2009)

Websites

www.avert.org

The website of Avert, an international AIDS charity.

www.globalhealth.org/hiv_aids

A website of the Global Health Council containing information about HIV/AIDS.

www.nhs.uk/conditions/HIV

A website of the UK National Health Service containing information about HIV/AIDS

www.who.int/hiv/en

A website of the World Health Organization describing the worldwide spread of HIV/AIDS, including statistics for each country.

www.youthaidscoalition.org

The website of GYCA, the Global Youth Coalition on HIV/AIDS.

Index

Page numbers in **bold** refer to pictures.

AIDS campaigners **25**
AIDS charities 10, 24, 25, 29, **39**
AIDS Drug Assistance Program 38
AIDS orphans 10, 12–15, 18–21, 22–25, **22–23**, 26, **27**, 32–35
ARV treatment 8–9, **9**, 10, 20, **20**, 21, 22–23, 24, **24**, 25, 29, 30, 31, **31**, 32, 35, 38, 42, 44
  side effects **24**
Australia 40–41
awareness, raising 10, 14–15, 25, **25**, 39

bereavement 9, 14, 32, 40
blood tests **9**, 22, 29, 30–31, **30**, 32
blood transfusions 7, 30
bullying 16–17, 34, **34**, 36

cancer 6, 12, 18, 32, 42, 44
care homes 19
cells 6
child carers 10, **11**, 26, 28, 29
condoms 10, 22, 30, 33, 35, 44
confiding in others 13, 14, 34, **34**, 41, 42, 43

dating 16, 41, 42–43
detention centres 36, 37, 38, 44
Diana, Princess of Wales **15**
diet, healthy 31, **31**
drug users 7, 9, 16, 23, 30, 36, 37, **37**, 42

education about HIV/AIDS 10, 15, 25, 32, 34, 35, 41, 42

education, missing out on 10, 24, 25, 26, 29, 32, 36

fever 8
foster homes 19, 20, 26, 41
foster parents 20–21, 40
France 7, 16–17

Gallo, Robert **6**

HAART 8–9, 20, 21, 44
haemophilia **39**, 44
hepatitis C 18, 44
Honduras 28–31

ignorance about HIV/AIDS 17, 25, 32, 33, 34, 35, **40**, 42
immune system 6, 8, 24, 31, 32, 38, 44
India 8

mother-to-child transmission 7, **7**, 10, 16, 22, 29, 32, 37, 40

needle-exchange programmes 9
needle sharing 7, 23, 30, 36, 37, **37**
Nigeria 8
nutrition 11, **31**

pneumonia 6, 12, 44
prejudice 14, 34, 38, **40**, 42, 44
prisons 22, 23
prostitution 26, 29

relationships 16, 17, 38, 41, **41**, 43
Ryan White Care Act 38, **39**

safe sex 7, 9, 10, 25, 30, 44
school 10, 11, 12, 15, 16, 17, **18–19**, 20, 24, 26, 29, 31, 32,

32–33, 34, 36, **39**, 42
sexual violence 23
Singapore 42–43
Siyaphila La HIV treatment programme **9**, **20**, **24**
skin, dry and flaky 22, 32
sore throat 8, 22
South Africa 7, 8, **9**, **20**, 22–25
South Asia 8
stigma about HIV/AIDS 13, 19, 26, 35, 36, 44
sub-Saharan Africa 8, 10, 22, 44
support, comfort and advice 13, 14, 16, 20–21, 25, 34, 38, **39**, 41
symptoms of HIV/AIDS 8–9, 12, 14, 22, 32, 44

tiredness 8, 12, **12–13**, 22, 25, 32
transmission of HIV 7, 15, 20, 25, 30, 37

United Kingdom 18–21
United States **6**, 7, 12–15, 32–39
unprotected sex 7, 22, 23, 24, 33, 37

viruses 6, 44

weight loss 8, 14
White, Ryan **39**

young people 9, 10, **11**, 13, 15, 22, 25, 26, 29, 32, 33, 35

Zambia 26, **27**
Zimbabwe 10–11